Princess Isabella and The Mystery of the Pink Dragon

Written by

K. B. Lebsock and Jessica Wulf

Tiny Princess Isabella was born in Wyoming, where there are open spaces, rolling hills, mountains and blue skies.

When she was old enough to leave her mama, Princess Isabella was adopted and she moved to her new home in a suburb of Denver, Colorado.

Joshua Tree Publishing
• Chicago •

JoshuaTreePublishing.com

ISBN: 978-0-9886577-7-9

Copyright © 2014 K. B. Lebsock and Jessica Wulf
All rights reserved. No part of this book may be reproduced or transmitted in any form or by any means, electronic or mechanical, including photocopying, recording or by any information storage and retrieval system without written permission from the authors.

Acknowledgments: Thanks to a dear departed friend, Marty Drucker, who planted the idea of a picture book featuring Isabella, and another dear friend, Nola VonEye. A very Special Thank You to Joyce and Dale Douglass. Thank you to Debbie Ecker, owner of It's A Dogs Life Dog Grooming Salon; Taami Bash, owner of Centerstage Starz; Ballet Teacher Gina Eslinger; Dancers Mia, Tahli, Arielle, Allison, Ysabel, Bethany; School Teacher Amber; School Children Keegan, Quint, Adrianna, Kailey Wilson, Tejada, Stephanie, Trinity Anderson, Skylar, Marta, and T.J.Gretz; Pom-Pom Coach Janay Lebsock; Doggie Friends Chica and Domino; and finally to the Trainers at the Aspen Grove Apple Store. Thanks also to Jessica's beloved children-friends Emma-Rae, Elias and Cora, and Isabella and Andrew. All of these children remind us of the beauty and wonder of our world when seen through the eyes of a child.

Photography: K. B. Lebsock

Printed in the United States of America

Isabella was sooo happy!

She had a soft pink bed to sleep in…

She was happiest at home, but she loved visiting Debbie the Dog Groomer and going to the dance studio for class and rehearsal...

and she even enjoyed attending school to study and to learn.

She especially loved pom-pom practice and to cheer at ball games.
GO TEAM GO!!!

AND, on top of all that, she had lots of toys to play with!

She didn't think her life could get any better because everything was perfect!

But then, one day Isabella was walking by her bed and she stopped, unable to believe her eyes!

There sat a beautiful Pink Dragon!

Isabella LOVED her new friend sooo much! Everywhere she went, so did Pink Dragon.

Pink Dragon even had breakfast, lunch, and dinner with Isabella...and slept with her in the soft bed.

Princess Isabella felt safe with Pink Dragon because she could tell Pink Dragon secrets, have talks with her, and dress her up in fun outfits.

Pink Dragon became Isabella's Best Friend.

One day, Isabella was sooo excited! Her family was going to take her to see *Toy Story*! She put on her coat and hat, and completely forgot about Pink Dragon until everyone else was ready to go.

Isabella felt sooo bad.

There wasn't time to put on Pink Dragon's coat and hat. Pink Dragon had to stay home all alone.

She looked sooo sad sitting by the lamp.

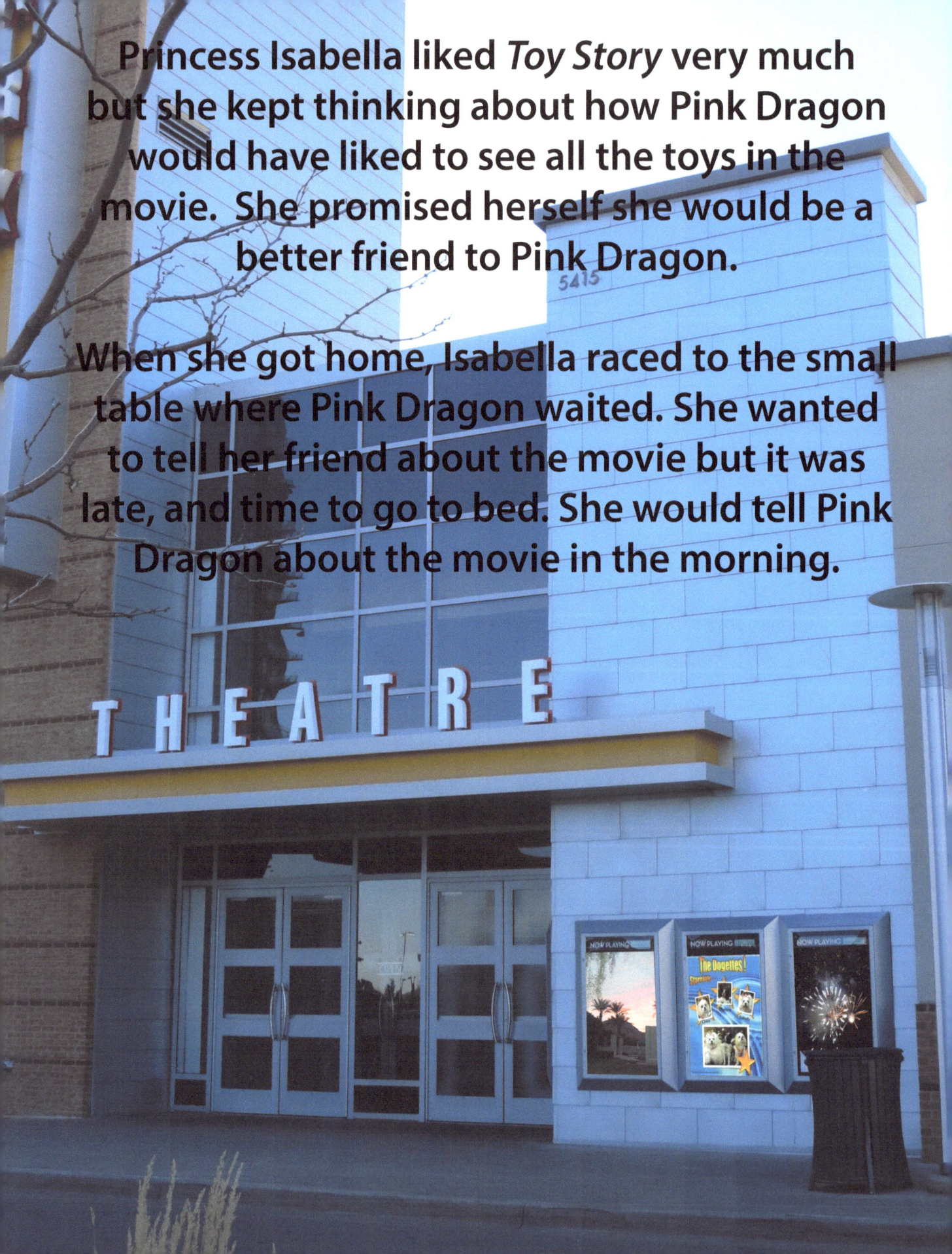

Princess Isabella liked *Toy Story* very much but she kept thinking about how Pink Dragon would have liked to see all the toys in the movie. She promised herself she would be a better friend to Pink Dragon.

When she got home, Isabella raced to the small table where Pink Dragon waited. She wanted to tell her friend about the movie but it was late, and time to go to bed. She would tell Pink Dragon about the movie in the morning.

Pink Dragon was still sleeping when Isabella awoke the next morning.

She hurried outside for her Daily Squirrel Patrol and was disappointed there were no squirrels. So she ran back inside, but when she reached the soft pink bed, she saw that…

OH, NO, NO, NO!!!

PINK DRAGON WAS GONE!!!

Where could Pink Dragon be?
Maybe in the kitchen for breakfast?

Sure enough, breakfast was in the bowl, but there was no sign of Pink Dragon. Isabella was so worried about Pink Dragon that she wasn't even hungry. But she knew it was important to eat a good breakfast, so she munched some kibble and thought about where Pink Dragon could be. Isabella was determined to search everywhere for her dear friend.

Isabella started looking in the house.

No, Pink Dragon was not in the house.

Next Princess Isabella searched the car—the front seat, under the seats, in the trunk, in all the door pockets, and even in Isabella's own car seat, where her family always made sure she was safely buckled in before the car moved. Pink Dragon was not in the car.

Even though Pink Dragon did not need to be groomed herself, maybe she had gone to visit Debbie the Groomer.

But no, Debbie had not seen Pink Dragon, and she gave Isabella a hug of encouragement.

The next place to look was the dance studio.

Pink Dragon was not there.
Now Isabella was really worried.
Where could her friend be?
The only place left to look was at the school.
So off she went to school.

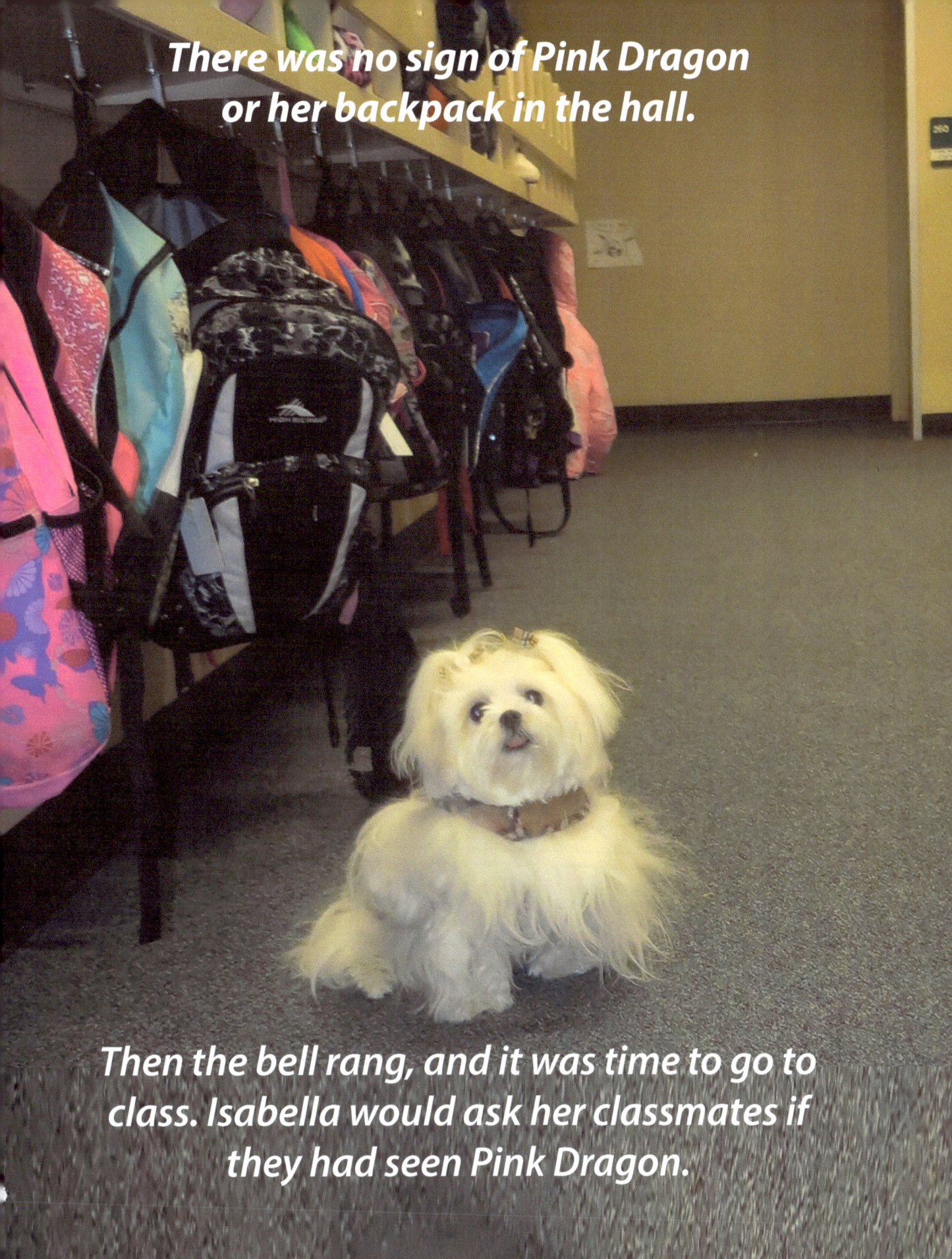

There was no sign of Pink Dragon or her backpack in the hall.

Then the bell rang, and it was time to go to class. Isabella would ask her classmates if they had seen Pink Dragon.

They had not seen Pink Dragon and promised to help look for her later.

For now, Isabella had to stop her search and listen to the teacher talk about geography. She tried to pay attention, but all she could think about was her missing friend.

Next came art class, and Isabella was the model.

And after that, when classes were finished for the day, the kids kept their promise to help look for Pink Dragon.

They searched all throughout the school, but they could not find her, and now it was time for pom-pom practice.

Maybe Pink Dragon was there!! Filled with new hope, Isabella quickly changed into her pom-pom outfit and raced to the sports field.

But Pink Dragon was not on the field, and Isabella was getting discouraged. Then she remembered that dragons like to hide under bleachers. THAT WAS IT!!! She was sooo sure Pink Dragon would be there, and she was sooo sad when she did not find her friend, not even with the help of Janay, her pom-pom coach.

Now all Isabella wanted to do was go home and sleep. But Janay persuaded her to stay for pom-pom practice even though she was sad; practice might help her feel better. Janay asked so nicely that Isabella agreed.

And it did turn out that Isabella felt a little better after practice, but now she was tired, sooo tired that she fell asleep in the car on the way home.

When she got home, the first thing Isabella did was invite her two friends, Domino and Chica, over for a visit. They knew Pink Dragon; maybe they had seen her. But her friends had not seen Pink Dragon that day. So Isabella told them the whole sad story. Domino and Chica felt sooo bad for Isabella!

Isabella asked Domino and Chica if they would help her search the house again, which her friends agreed to do. The three doggies searched, sooo carefully, but they could not find Pink Dragon.

By then it was close to dinner time, and Domino and Chica had to go home. On the way out the door, Domino asked if there was any place in the house that had not been searched, such as places where Pink Dragon had never gone before. Isabella thought about that as she waved goodbye to her friends.

It was true she hadn't searched the bedroom closet, under the bed, or the bathtub. Why Pink Dragon would be in any of those places Isabella could not imagine, but she decided that after dinner she would look anyway, just in case.

Isabella ate her dinner very fast, then started her search:
in the bedroom closet…
under the bed…
in the bathtub…

NO PINK DRAGON.

Isabella was very sad. If she didn't find Pink Dragon by bedtime, she'd have to sleep in the soft pink bed all by herself. Just the thought made her feel lonely.

Then, from the laundry room down the hall, she heard a soft ding noise and knew the dryer had stopped.

WAIT!

The laundry room! She hadn't checked the laundry room! Isabella rushed down the hall. And when she turned through the doorway, she saw that the dryer door was open, and, and…

OH, YES, YES, YES!!! THERE SHE WAS!!!

Pink Dragon was all warm and soft, and smelled sooo good. She'd had a bath! That's where she'd been all day! A wash in the machine and then a Dry and Fluff, much like Isabella did at Debbie the Groomer's.

THE MYSTERY WAS SOLVED!!!

Isabella and Pink Dragon snuggled under the froggie blankie in the soft pink bed and talked. Isabella promised to be a better friend to Pink Dragon and to always leave enough time to prepare for their outings. She would love and watch over Pink Dragon the way her family loved and watched over her.

Isabella and Pink Dragon promised they would be…

Friends Forever!

THE END

www.ingramcontent.com/pod-product-compliance
Lightning Source LLC
Chambersburg PA
CBHW041119300426
44112CB00002B/34